Asperity Street

ASPERITY STREET

POEMS BY
Gail White

ABLE MUSE PRESS

Printed in the United States of America

Library of Congress Control Number: 2015936196

ISBN 978-1-927409-54-1 (paperback)
ISBN 978-1-927409-55-8 (digital)

Cover image: "Erkanmatik 2014 06" by Erkan Kalenderli

Cover & book design by Alexander Pepple

Able Muse Press is an imprint of *Able Muse:* A Review of Poetry, Prose & Art—at
www.ablemuse.com

Able Muse Press
467 Saratoga Avenue #602
San Jose, CA 95129

Acknowledgments

I am grateful to the editors of the following journals where many of the poems in this collection originally appeared, sometimes in earlier versions:

14 by 14, Able Muse, Alabama Literary Review, American Arts Quarterly, Angle, Anglican Theological Review, Blue Unicorn, Chimaera, Chronicles, Crab Creek Review, Evansville Review, First Things, Iambs & Trochees, Light Quarterly, The Lyric, Measure, Mezzo Cammin, Raintown Review, Soundzine, Tar River Poetry, Think Journal, Verse Wisconsin.

Foreword

Gail White has done it again: here is another collection by one of America's wittiest, most technically adept, funniest and most serious commentators on what it feels like to be human. *Asperity Street*—the latest title in a distinguished bibliography that includes the full-length collections *The Price of Everything, Easy Marks;* the anthology *Kiss and Part;* and the chapbooks *Women & Other Cynics, Poets & Such, Ignoble Truths, Gail White: Greatest Hits 1981-2001*—features all of the intelligence, cold-eyed objectivity and verbal delights that readers expect from its author, but, as always, challenges the reader with quirky surprises.

The organizing framework, this time, is the conventional Seven Ages of Man, which the poet has reduced (wisely, I think: I've always found seven too many!) to four, and titled "Growing," "Working," "Holding," and "Leaving." It is orderly and almost too respectably traditional at first glance: but this is Gail White, after all, and the surprises that subvert the reader's expectations begin at once.

For instance, in the opening section, "Growing," the first poem is titled "The Prison" and announces immediately that "childhood is wretched," proving it in language we recognize as adolescent: "you" means kids, the helpless, moneyless, carless victims of those who never believe "your heart can break." The tone tells us that these poems are not simply going to comment on the separate stages of life, but intend, rather, to take us into those stages, whether that involves time travel back to what we've left or forward to what we have not yet entered. The final stanza, which begins with "Escape as best you can," suggests several melodramatic escapes, and ends with "At any price, grow tall." The humor resides in the distance in time between reader and speaker, and leaves us wondering if the "prison" referred to is childhood itself, or the child's mind that equates happiness with total autonomy or recognition by "taller gods."

No sooner does the reader find himself in the second poem, however, than the point of view changes, and the "prison" with it. The speaker says, with what sounds like the condescension of those "taller gods" for whom even the young "nurselet" is barely worthy of respect:

> The babies seem alike as geese.
> I hardly know which one's my niece,
> until a nurselet points her out. . . .

But then, having discovered the newly born "comma in the human race," the view shifts to the creature herself, now regarded affectionately, until the shocking close:

> . . . how tenderly we'll bend above
> the small cloaca that we love.

The tenderness constitutes one surprise, but that "cloaca," a term borrowed from the anatomy of animals, or urban sanitation, feels like a brick thrown through the window of our consciousness: yes, the infants we love are small animals, and so are we. And now we know that these poems are not going to leave us alone to enjoy the fulfillment of our expectations: they're going to hit us, as they say, "where we live," as in "Nostalgia for an Old Religion," in which the religion longed for is nothing less than the pagan magical thinking native to the human race but anathema to "sterner deities" whose "talk was all of Death and Sin."

The rest of "Growing" invites us through Southern social history and its living legacy, ambivalent memories of family members and the certainties they lived by, losses and grudges, quarrels with religion, marriage, and the literary treasures that enshrine the values of the tribe. The section ends with a quick backward look in an unforgettable poem titled "Old Photographs" that ends with "I've come to love these strangers, now they're dead." And then, on to "Haunted," which doesn't deny that love but cuts it with acid:

> My mother was burned, not buried,
> as if we were afraid that she
> would rise up out of a concrete vault
> and trouble her family.

Part 2, "Working," reflects the mind of the effective adult in the world: it's a cultivated mind that expresses itself through references to the shared experiences of the speaker's generation and responds to figures from history, art, mythology and science, including Emily Dickinson, Jeremy Bentham and Saint John of the Cross. In the very first poem, "A Rolling Stone Gathers Wisdom," a takeoff on Housman's "When I Was One-and-Twenty," the speaker is sixty-five and looking back on a life of changes. But unlike the *carpe diem* we expect, what we get is contentment, a settled appreciation of what life is and isn't at that stage, and the almost-placid comment that "... I've got lots of time."

The concerns tackled in this section include making it in the world without expecting too much, inhabiting that world without doing too much damage, marrying without incurring a disaster like poor Emma Bovary, and—the religious element through the eyes of this particular speaker—being Mary and surviving the difficulties created and borne by your son, the prophet and carpenter. The voice of the teacher makes itself heard in this section, in a magnificent sonnet. The teacher asks St. John, patron saint of poets, to illuminate the minds of her students, who have been assigned his "Dark Night of the Soul," but interpret that masterpiece as an adulterous adventure:

> . . . My best student bets
> her husband locks her out. I tried to check
> these thoughts by pointing to her night of bliss
> under the cypress trees, but they were cold
> to ecstasy—young puritans who kiss
> in condoms nowadays. And when I told
> them who you were, it didn't change their minds.
> Please help me tell them what the starlight finds.

The themes have darkened, but paradoxically the tone has lightened, which helps to confirm what I've thought for some time now: that the darkest corners of life are often explored most accurately by the so-called "light verse" poets whose exuberant gift for effortless form teaches them to be nimble with matter as well as manner.

The section ends with the appearance of the cat, Gail White's tutelary spirit, in "She Compares Her Lover to Her Cat," which sets up a series of contrasts and closes with this:

> The panther only purrs—but you, my mate,
> how can you be so damned articulate
> yet lack the sense to come in when it rains?
> If only you had fur and she had brains.

Section 3, "Holding," opens with the wholly unexpected: "sudden joy" over the most ordinary pleasures, including nature, books, art, a marriage that works, friendship. "Is this contentment?" asks this new voice. And it answers itself: "Yes. Well, I'll be damned."

Now the reader's attention is drawn to the artistry of the work, and to its richness and universality. Poem after poem, in glorious imagery and dramatic episodes, draws the reader outside of himself, into a room in Pompeii to join, "in an iron carapace/ of ashes," a maid and the child she attempted to save; into the ruins of a beloved restaurant destroyed by Katrina, where the speaker begs for "shining dishes" full of "my weekly miracle of loaves and fishes"; to the silence of Mesa Verde, in stately language that honors those who vanished there, as we will, someday, vanish somewhere.

The voice speaking this section takes pride in what it knows it is doing very well, and is not above drawing attention to, for example, a perfect villanelle that begins:

> The world does not need one more villanelle,
> yet teachers still assign the exercise.
> Sooner or later someone does it well.

The variations of that second repetend are, by themselves, worth the price of the book, and so is the self-conscious sonnet in the voice of a fortune-teller (a figure Gail White has used before), who proffers answers to many questions presumably asked by the customer, and ends with this brusque dismissal:

> In late July, beware of traffic fines.
> That's it. You've only paid for fourteen lines.

This is poetry having fun, doing what art does at its best, telling the truths it wants to tell in its own way, almost showing off as it leads us where it thinks we need to go. The section ends—and effectively begins the next—with "The Table of Antique Postcards": a poem that begins with the admittedly "trivial views" and "trite messages" we send home from our travels, as we read them over the speaker's shoulder. The poem ends with this:

> . . . Here are
> the proofs, the tiny slanting blue-black trails
>
> that led them to the columbarium
> where lie the grateful dead. X marks my room.

Now we're ready for Part 4, appropriately titled "Leaving," in which the tone darkens, the matter deepens, and the manner shrinks to match the few options left in the speaker's personal (imagined) future.

The vocabulary becomes medical, familiar to readers in our eighties and beyond: such terms as "memory aids," "diagnosis" and "post-diagnosis," "Alzheimer's" and "hospice" create the atmosphere, and poem after poem deals with the complex plight of the widowed and soon-to-be-widowed. The surprises are still there, but subtler now, and awash in references—tender but ungilded by sentiment—to the body, whether actual or remembered.

Among the most startling poems in the collection, the monorhyme that opens this section, "Limits of My Knowledge," consists of ten lines in language so stripped down that they hardly seem the work of the same poet whose intricate formal verse glittered only a page or two ago. It merits total inclusion here:

> Along the beach the footprints wend.
> I do not know where things will end.
>
> You found yourself another friend.
> I do not know why things must end.
>
> Researchers tell us time can bend.
> I do not know when things will end.
>
> The plots of all the movies blend.
> I do not know how things will end.
>
> I've seen the way my white cells trend.
> I only know that things will end.

Now the work traces relentless losses, beginning with the loss of interest in or desire for experience:

My heart, an old and tired cat,
surveying age's box of toys,
will not uncurl itself for that.

And almost equally painful, the loss of independence, in terms familiar to those of us who have cared for elderly parents:

These are the things I need to say
To sound as usual on the phone.
The longer I keep my child at bay,
The longer my life is still my own.

The bereaved leave letters to the dead "among the twisted roots of an oak tree," make the bed now used on one side alone, learn to care for themselves, and even find uses for the empty closet space.

Little by little humor finds its back door into these views of the inevitable, and finally, in the quiet, highly visual tercets of the closing poem, so does acceptance:

Whatever good we might have done
is like the prints where foxes run,
lost when the snow melts in the sun.

. . .

The work of all our lifetime lets
us look on death with no regrets:
we vanish as the snow forgets.

So much better, wiser, and more generous than "raging against" anything at all! *Asperity Street,* which surprises at the end by doing exactly what its premise predicts and ending with the close of life—an obedient capitulation nobody expects from Gail White!—comes down, at the end, on the value of what remains after us, unchanged by our absence.

Brava, poet, for leading us to face that absence with equanimity and grace, and for giving the reader so much pleasure in the contemplation of what we experienced when we were those other, younger people, and have always been in the daily process of leaving.

—Rhina P. Espaillat

Contents

Part IV.   LEAVING

Asperity Street

PART I.   GROWING

The Prison

Childhood is wretched, even if you're not
abused and have no scars to show in court.
Children are powerless and moneyless
and worst of all, they're short.

You have no transportation. Taller gods
carry you where they will. You have to go
to schools, to doctors, other children's parties,
powerless to say no.

No one believes your heart can really break.
No one respects the thoughts you bring from school.
Be cute, believe in Santa Claus, they'll laugh
and hug their little fool.

Escape as best you can. Jump from a cliff,
swim through a river, scale the prison wall,
run through a forest fighting off wild beasts.
At any price, grow tall.

Looking through the Nursery Window

The babies seem alike as geese.
I hardly know which one's my niece,
until a nurselet points her out
and demonstrates she's blonde and stout.
One of a thousand—just a space
and comma in the human race—
but when we find her thrashing, wet
and howling in her bassinet,
how tenderly we'll bend above
the small cloaca that we love.

Nostalgia for an Old Religion

The Easter Rabbit came again
each April, bearing candy eggs,
marshmallow Peeps, and pictures drawn
inside a box of painted dregs
from the refiner's sugar bin.
When I woke up, he'd come and gone.
I never knew how he got in.

In those lost days a fairy came
and gathered up the missing teeth
I carefully placed underneath
my pillow, paying for the same
in shiny dimes. Her lovely game
consoled me for my toothless grin.
I never knew how she got in.

But chief of all this joyous crew
was Santa Claus. Eight reindeer drew
him down to Earth on Christmas Eve.
He always left me toys galore
(whatever I had asked him for)—
who wouldn't wonder, and believe?
But since our roof was solid tin,
I never knew how he got in.

When I grew up, the books I read
killed all the old enchantment dead.
I studied new theologies
with older, sterner deities
who had no cash or candy eggs
and never came on reindeer legs.
Their talk was all of Death and Sin.
I never knew how those got in.

On Asperity Street

My deep Southern family
all loved to eat:
Thanksgiving dinners
and barbecued wieners
and fish fries with hush puppies
in summer's heat.
We were just middle class
but we made both ends meet
and we put on no airs
but we did have our pride
and nothing to hide
on Asperity Street.

Our patriotism
did not need a push
below Mason-Dixon—
we voted for Nixon,
we voted for Bush
(even W. Bush).
We didn't drive Cadillacs,
didn't wear fur,
but all of us knew
who our ancestors were.
Adultery always
was very discreet
and no one was gay
(or at least didn't say)

and our drunks drank at home
on Asperity Street.

We respected ourselves
when our fortune went smash
and we looked down on people
who couldn't pay cash.
We gave up our steaks
but we still paid the rent
and the government (Yanks)
never gave us a cent.
Whatever our plight
we stood on our own feet.
We looked out for ourselves
and owed nobody thanks,
but formed into ranks
of the Christian and white,
the politically right
and the forces of light
on Asperity Street.

My Personal Recollections of
Not Being Asked to the Prom

I never minded my unpopularity
in those days. Books were friends and poets (dead)
were lovers. Brainy girls were still a rarity,
and boys preferred big bosoms to well-read
and saucy wits. I look back now with pity
on the young Me I didn't pity then.
I didn't know that I was almost pretty
and might have had a charm for older men.

And my poor mom, who never bought a fluffy
ball gown or showed me how to dress my hair,
she must have wondered where she got this stuffy
daughter. She didn't say it, but her stare
asked whether genes or nurture were to blame.
(But I got married, Mother, all the same.)

Brother and Sister

Cat-quick and scalpel-sharp, the wit
that flashes out between these two.
Each knows the tender spot to hit,
which made-up memories are true.

The family learns to bob and weave,
letting them keep the ring alone,
knowing that not a guest will leave
until their mocking scrapes the bone.

Explorers venturing undismayed
to join these two as man or wife
will find their bodies ready flayed
by love that wields a hunting knife.

Thérèse of Lisieux

At fifteen she was beating on the door
of Carmel, hounding the Pope to let her in,
though she was underage. He let her win.
Who knew that she would die at twenty-four?
She might have lived till eighty, carrying
that adolescent torch for Jesus Christ,
the only man she thought worth marrying.
She would have been his sister, been his priest,
been anything the stodgy rules allowed.
What they allowed was cold that chilled her lungs
and brought the taste of blood to burn her tongue,
laying the body low but not the proud
spirit that beat on doors until the day
love opened them and took her breath away.

A Speech for Juliet's Nurse

All lovers need a friend with sense
to point their follies out to them—
as Romeo in haste runs hence
to plant four melons on one stem.

Ephemeral as the glowworm's shine,
love changes with the time of day.
What's Juliet more than Rosaline,
when in the dark all cats are gray?

All he, in his defense, can say
is that love covers all his sins,
while she, my girl, prepares to play
a losing game until she wins.

As friend and nurse and raconteur,
I'm in her confidence, and so
I'll get to listen at the door.
I'm up to all the tricks they know,

unless—unless there's something here
that outlasts midnight's lingering.
But dawn will cure them, never fear.
These lovers only want one thing.

Astrolabe

Is that a name to give your only son?
What did you care? My mother loved you so
she threw off beauty and became a nun
only because you said, "It's over. Go,
you bride of Christ, we're only siblings now."
I never saw you save by fits and starts
and poor relations raised me, God knows how—
in wedlock born, a bastard in your hearts.
True, mother found me a small benefice
which kept me in the church, and therefore near
to her, but never near enough to kiss,
or talk with no one else to overhear.
Her love, your life, remained a world apart.
It took the pair of you to break my heart.

Nativity Scene

She has no privacy, but doesn't mind,
since everything is upside down today.
Even the cow is unsurprised to find
a useless infant in the useful hay.
For shepherds on the hills, a filigree
quartet of angels dances in the sky.
Painters will love this story. They can see
unbodied beings with an artist's eye.
For most of us our death will cancel birth.
Who cares how popes and presidents are born?
But now three kings adore on Middle Earth
a wonder that exceeds the unicorn.
Nothing is changed, yet everything is new:
some stories look so strange they might be true.

Old Photographs

Here is my mother, smiling, very chic,
come from the alien North at twenty-two
to see her married brother for a week,
but the week turned to months (as weeks will do)
while suitors flocked around. My father, who
was poorest of the lot, prevailed at last,
and when I asked her why, she said, "I knew
that he'd be good to me." Fixed in the past,
I see a couple in their wedding clothes,
a Navy man in uniform, a queen
of Carnival. I see them at the Rose
Parade, the Derby, two that might have seen
the world together. They raised me instead.
I've come to love these strangers, now they're dead.

Haunted

My mother was burned, not buried,
as if we were afraid that she
would rise up out of a concrete vault
and trouble her family.

We didn't choose any garments
to be worn to the end of time.
Her jewelry was shared out equally
among her sisters and mine.

There was no religious service,
and no ridiculous wake.
Nobody brought us food or flowers
or had any coffee and cake.

We burned her body's corruption
in a pure white seamless flame.
We didn't bury my mother,
but she's walking just the same.

Part II.   WORKING

A Rolling Stone Gathers Wisdom

When I was five-and-thirty,
I thought that I was old,
my waist no longer sylph-like,
my hair no longer gold.
'Twas useless to console me,
or offer me champagne,
for I was five-and-thirty,
and death was on my brain.

When I was five-and-forty,
my heart was full of fears.
When I was five-and-fifty,
I would not count the years.
But there've been subtle changes
in Nature's paradigm—
now I am five-and-sixty,
and I've got lots of time.

Gossip

Her wedding dress was crumpled on the floor
like tissue paper, like the dead white flowers
for the reception. And they searched for hours,
called the police, and then sent out for more
hard liquor. And her husband took the train
through every state that bordered Tennessee.
They say his hair turned white at twenty-three
and no one ever saw his wife again.

Well you can just imagine what was said—
the usual when someone disappears—
abduction, rape, and left somewhere for dead.
But not a trace of her was found. And years
went by with no solution. But her maid
of honor used to say (choking back tears)
"She was afraid, poor thing. Just so afraid."

When Jesus Was Grown

His mother breathed a deep sigh of relief
when he turned twenty-five and nothing strange
had happened. (Maybe it was all a dream,
that business with the angel.)

She might yet manage to arrange a match
with some nice Jewish girl—it was high time
and then she could relax, look forward to
a few polite grandchildren.

But though he was the finest carpenter
for miles around, had really learned the trade,
and knew and loved the Torah, nonetheless,
she had concerns about him.

He seemed too fond of prophecies about
the world turned upside down, and although she
was charitable to a fault, she felt
he loved the poor to excess.

And there were rumors of a prophet now
who lived on locusts in the wilderness.
His message was outrageous, and she hoped
her son would never hear it.

To Jeremy Bentham

Across the bayou, where for twenty years
I faced a jungle, vines and cypress knees,
this morning, realizing my worst fears,
an iron claw is pulling up the trees.
Houses will come, and cars and SUVs,
as nature yields to stronger human force,
making a habitat for families
with children, birthdays, marriage and divorce.

So, Bentham, everything is for the best,
and where wild creatures nested in the wood
the human race will build a different nest,
serving the greater number's greater good.
How happy must the lovely families be
to compensate the hawks, the ducks, and me.

Boomers on a Cruise

Everything, O monks, is burning.
　　　—Buddha

The isles of Greece, the isles of Greece,
where we've obtained on credit cards
one tapestry of silky fleece,
two icons, three amphora shards.

Two noble truths: that life is pain
and that our cravings are the cause.
But here we've all grown young again
and laughter routs the cosmic laws.

On Delos, once a treasure town,
gray lizards flick the drying dust,
where once ambitious Greeks burned down
in anger, ignorance, and lust.

Our ocean-going steel cocoon
spins out the silk of innocence.
Only the water and the moon
bring whispers of impermanence.

On Santorini, once the home
of vampires, we look out to sea
from underneath a bluer dome,
and call this noon eternity.

The sun melts down in tropic gold
like Strega in a cocktail glass.
The moon and moon-drawn tides are old
and, like the dinosaurs, shall pass.

We build up shelves against the tide:
our luxuries, our workout tapes.
But slowly we burn down inside,
and find there are no fire escapes.

Mating

What is it that compels the fish
to fertilize the female's eggs,
lying in glossy globules, bright
below the tide-pool's slimy edge?

It can't be love. It probably
can't even be called instinct, quite.
Respect, perhaps, as they glide on,
equal with equal, past the site.

Work

It's only artists and the very rich
who work for the sheer love of what they do.
Most jobs are rounds of routine boredom which
set up the hoops we all keep jumping through
just for the food and drink that make us strong
enough to jump through the same hoops again
tomorrow and tomorrow, for as long
as we have health enough. For work-bound men
and women, the Vacation looms above
their cubicles like man's lost paradise.
It passes with a breath, and then we move
through our old maze like laboratory mice.
This is the tragedy we all rehearse,
the blight that man was born for, Adam's curse.

Woman into Tree

Greek myth records the known (but hated) fact
that women do not always want men's love.
Some, in the struggle to avoid the act
and keep their would-be mates at one remove,
have called on heaven to destroy their shape.
Most were not answered. Many were betrayed.
But lucky Daphne spoiled Apollo's rape:
her lips grew rough, bark-covered as they prayed;
her raised arms stiffened into boughs to sift
white blossoms on the god's defeated pride.
How many girls inherited the gift
of Daphne? Under flowering lips they hide
the bitter taste of bark, and no one sees
how many sweet words fall from walking trees.

The Solitary Woman

In a pale pink shotgun house in Marigny,
Miz Hillman lived alone. Nobody came
to see her and she had no family,
so, week by week her life was much the same:
she went to church and said the rosary,
took in the mail for neighbors out of town,
adopted cats, watched MSNBC,
and at a rolltop desk she wrote things down—
things no one ever saw, although we guessed
a novel, memoirs, poetry, and more.
We spied no papers though we did our best.
And when she died alone, at eighty-four,
with no companion but a big gray cat,
we pitied her. We were such fools as that.

Postcard to Miss Dickinson

I'm Somebody? Well, no,
Perhaps a half one, though,
While you've been somebody for years—
Perhaps you didn't know?

How dreary to be Nobody!
How fetid, like the Bog
Where chortling frogs exult above
The stifled Pollywog!

I Come to the Garden

I can name so few flowers. This is why
I'm not a better poet. Shakespeare knew
oxlip and gillyvor and eglantine,
while I, beyond camellia, violet, rose,
and lily am reduced to saying "There,
those crinkly yellow things!" Out on a walk
with mad John Clare, I'd learn a dozen names
for plants, and bless the wonders underfoot.
"More servants wait on man," George Herbert said,
"than he'll take notice of." He's right again,
of course. I've never had observant eyes.
Would I care more if my heart's soil were deep
enough for flowers and loves to take firm root?
Mine is a gravel garden, where the rake
does all the cultivation I can take.

Dear Juan de la Cruz

I gave my class your "dark night" poem to read,
not telling them who wrote it. They were quick
to name adultery as the midnight deed
the female speaker runs to, in a thick
burqa of darkness. And the poor thing gets
her just deserts, being wounded in the neck
by a vampire lover. My best student bets
her husband locks her out. I tried to check
these thoughts by pointing to her night of bliss
under the cypress trees, but they were cold
to ecstasy—young puritans who kiss
in condoms nowadays. And when I told
them who you were, it didn't change their minds.
Please help me tell them what the starlight finds.

Ballade of Madame Bovary

Was it for this I learned to read
and write and bake a cherry pie?
I was romantic. "All I need
is love!" was my incessant cry.
But girls, however hard you try,
how long you work, how much you fret,
you'll meet the same reward as I—
a country doctor's all you get.

A wife is only fit to breed
her brats and sing their lullaby.
Oh, had I only given heed
to those sweet nuns who glorify
the Lord in prayer, and daily die,
I might have been a virgin yet.
But marriage makes the world a sty—
a country doctor's all you get.

I learned to do adultery's deed:
I took two lovers, one a sly
and skillful horseman (I the steed
he rode with such an expert thigh).
My second love was sweetly shy,
an easy fish in rapture's net.
But when I needed cash—good-bye!
A country doctor's all you get.

L'Envoi

Girls, never raise your hopes too high.
Lower your standards, and forget
you meant to catch a rich man's eye—
a country doctor's all you get.

The Girls Who Got Ahead

When all the bright young women studied law
and medicine, I thought a PhD
in Women and the Novel would unthaw
the frozen heart of Academe for me.

When all the bright girls married, where was I?
Still shacking up with poets that I met
in bars, convinced that genius and rye
would write us into fame and out of debt.

The bright girls made investments by the rules.
I kept on writing novels in my mind.
They sent their handsome kids to private schools
and I became the girl they left behind.

Bright girls got married and ahead and rich,
while I keep waiting for the ride to hitch.

She Compares Her Lover to Her Cat

While you're away, my love, I stroke instead
of you the dainty panther in my bed,
more exquisite than satin and more sleek
than rain, but sadly unequipped to speak.
You are my information source, my song,
my lover's lexicon—and yet how wrong
about your health, how vexed with all I write,
how testy at an unintended slight!
The panther only purrs—but you, my mate,
how can you be so damned articulate
yet lack the sense to come in when it rains?
If only you had fur and she had brains.

Part III.   HOLDING

Sudden Euphoria of
a Middle-Aged Southerner

Youth gone and beauty never having come
nor money either, where's it springing from,
this sudden joy? Fine weather and the slope
of green lawn to the bayou, snow-white shape
of heron fishing on the bank, is part
of it. The rest is books and art,
good health, two cats, a marriage going strong
for twenty years, a friendship just as long,
plus writing, and the love of what I write.

Summing up joys, I savor my delight:
this is as close as I will ever get
to the mystic's peak of holy self-forget-
fulness, the warrior in his savage bliss,
the lover's ecstasy. I'll stop with this—
a sense of living in a world well-planned.
Is this contentment? Yes. Well, I'll be damned.

Tourist in India

Monkeys are urban animals in Delhi,
peacocks are city birds. And everywhere,
I'm drowned in waves of men who want to sell me
overpriced souvenirs. I fight for air

and reach the marble shores of my hotel.
Thank God for Lutyens! Where would Delhi be
without the British? They used power well,
spread English, trained the boys that serve my tea.

But O seductive East! Today I found
a Hindu temple, entered and was crowned
with marigolds, made puja, walked around
a lingam thrice and sang "Jai Hanuman"
while monkeys chattered, and without a sound,
my Christian ghost indulgently looked on.

Crouching Female Figure: Pompeii

At first they were not much afraid,
but hour by hour the ashes fell,
layer on layer overlaid—
the soft gray snow that falls in hell.

When panic came, her mistress said,
"Lucilla, take the child and run."
But when she stumbled, both were dead.
Ashes had eaten up the sun.

Now, in an iron carapace
of ashes, here she crouches still,
shielding in vain her charge's face
while tourists photograph their fill.

Could God explain in layman's terms
what vices necrotized Pompeii,
when urban gods and rustic herms
were ashes in a single day?

No law, no logic eases pain
or stops the tidal wave of death.
Sinai and Etna both can rain
ashes that suffocate our breath.

Money Song

Money won't buy you the moon and stars,
but trips abroad and enormous cars
and fancy drinks in exclusive bars,
can all be purchased with money.

Money won't buy you wisdom and truth
or permanent beauty or lasting youth,
but it makes a very good substituth,
which makes it nice to have money.

The dog and the cat that you adore—
money won't make them love you more,
but it keeps the wolf away from the door,
which is why I wish I had money.

I'd have a fabulous London flat,
a house in Provence and a Persian cat,
and I'd give up being a Democrat,
if only I had enough money.

When all the sins of excessive wealth
had left me ruined, by speed or stealth,
I'd still have memories of my health,
and the fun I had with my money.

On the Death by Drowning of
My Favorite New Orleans Restaurant

The corner of Canal and Carrollton
sheltered Mandina's, where for seventeen
years every Saturday they poured me one
black Russian followed by trout amandine

or the best shrimp loaf on the whole Gulf coast.
But now the watermark is at my eyes,
the floors have rotted, and the stolid ghost
of a decayed refrigerator lies

prone on the sidewalk. And I'm shedding tears
over a stack of dishes, one of which
I'll steal in memory of those seventeen years
that made their gumbo and my life so rich.

Come back, my love! Serve me on shining dishes
my weekly miracle of loaves and fishes.

Song from Exile

When I lived in New Orleans,
my bridges all were burned
as was the candle at both ends
on drunken nights with artsy friends,
and far away in Florida
my mother grew concerned.

For drinking in New Orleans
was not a simple thing.
We lay head-downward on the stairs
and plotted books and love affairs,
and on the stroke of twelve o'clock
we'd pour a toast and sing.

The singing in New Orleans
was of extensive range:
from limericks to Russian chants,
and if a singer dropped his pants
or fainted in the fireplace,
we never thought it strange.

And since I left New Orleans
my time is largely spent
in being bored and drinking Cokes
and telling old New Orleans jokes,
and far away in Florida
my mother is content.

A Spin of the Prayer Wheel

— for Timothy Murphy

Hunter, when you are pursued,
kneel and let the hounds go past.
All our demons, first and last,
fear the scent of solitude.

As the lamas of Tibet
fling paper horses in the air
to rescue pilgrims from despair
when caught in winter's wiry net,

so take from me, a distant friend
who cannot reach you at your source,
the courage in a paper horse
that counsels you to rest and mend.

Though the winter chills you numb,
let the demon hounds race through.
Strength is storing up for you.
Hunter, you will overcome.

Prayer for Good Fortune

How do I know, when silent emptiness
is all I meet, that I'm not talking to
myself, just trying vainly to impress
the void? In short, how do I know there's You?
Lovers when kept apart send cards and gifts,
spend costly hours on the telephone,
will run together through all risks, all shifts—
will You? Or can You? Or am I alone
like Earth among the planets, sending out
my frantic signal, seeking a reply
from wiser, older worlds? How quench the doubt
that You may not be You but only I?
How can I know You love unless You pour
out miracles? How can I not crave more?

Statues of Antinous

are everywhere and you run into them
in unexpected places—Amsterdam,
New York, Vienna—where you recognize
a teenage boy who might have taken off
his clothes to change for soccer, with a mop
of curly hair all brushed one way, a nose
like Nefertiti's, and a sulky mouth:
you'd know him anywhere, as if you'd seen
his photograph, as if he might turn up
delivering a pizza. While you might
walk by Saint Paul and never notice him,
you can't miss young Antinous. And not
because he did a single thing. He simply caught
the emperor's eye. His immortality
was Hadrian's love. With cities, obelisks,
and marble busts, the emperor deified
a face that still lays criticism flat.
Does anyone love you as much as that?

A Crisis in Mesa Verde

The gatherers have gone away,
picked up their baskets and departed.
Hunters huddle in dismay.
The gatherers have gone away,
just leaving bread for one more day.
No hearth is swept, no fire started.
The gatherers have gone away,
picked up their baskets and departed.

The hunters put aside their spears
and look around them, disbelieving.
Gatherers fed the tribe for years.
The hunters lay aside their spears
and try to calm the children's fears
while wondering who will do the weaving.
Hunters put aside their spears
and look around them, disbelieving.

Slowly the pile of bones will rise,
the children drift away unheeded.
Could it have happened otherwise?
Slowly the pile of bones will rise,
the clothes wear out, the vats draw flies.
The hot clay ovens won't be needed.
Slowly the pile of bones will rise,
the children drift away unheeded.

50

No one will know in years to come
what happened here in bygone ages.
The land that knew them will be dumb.
No one will know in years to come
if death came soon and found them numb
or took them off in easy stages.
And who will care in years to come
what happened here in bygone ages?

Superfluous Words

The world does not need one more villanelle,
yet teachers still assign the exercise.
Sooner or later someone does it well.

More verses than the damned can read in hell
are written daily, so it's no surprise
the world does not need one more villanelle,

but does it need the countless things we sell
in stores, the million things we advertise?
Sooner or later something is done well.

The lovers meet, the monk prays in his cell,
the married have their kids whose scratchy cries
the world does not need. One more villanelle

or less, what does it matter? Truth to tell,
we all make things for others to despise.
Sooner or later someone does it well.

What if we fail in trying to excel?
We'll all fill coffins of a standard size.
The world does not need one more villanelle,
but still, from time to time, one does it well.

Sonnet

In Answer to Your Questions

Your Uncle Harry doesn't know himself
where he left the will. You've tried his desk? The dresser?
the farthest reaches of the kitchen shelf?
The dead are under a great deal of stress,

and they forget. As for your other question—
whether you'll find true love—Venus and Mars
are conjoined over Pisces, which suggests an
absolute negative on singles bars.

It's a good year for travel, cooking classes,
learning the waltz and the electric slide.
Go where the people are. Going to Mass is
recommended if you've never tried.

In late July, beware of traffic fines.
That's it. You've only paid for fourteen lines.

The Table of Antique Postcards

So many trivial views, so many trite
messages: "Finally made it to the Fair."
"This is our ship." "X marks my room." "Last night
we saw the Grateful Dead." With here and there

a "Happy Birthday." "I love Grandma." "Love
from Kansas City." "Love you—coming home."
Who knew the middle class had so much love
to scatter on these bits of polychrome?

Maybe they left home once and got as far
as Canada. Maybe they rode the rails
or took a cruise (this is our ship). Here are
the proofs, the tiny slanting blue-black trails

that led them to the columbarium
where lie the grateful dead. X marks my room.

PART IV.　　　　　　　LEAVING

Limits of My Knowledge

Along the beach the footprints wend.
I do not know where things will end.

You found yourself another friend.
I do not know why things must end.

Researchers tells us time can bend.
I do not know when things will end.

The plots of all the movies blend.
I do not know how things will end.

I've seen the way my white cells trend.
I only know that things will end.

The Way It Ended

So time went by and they were middle-aged,
which seemed a crazy joke that time had played
on two young lovers. They were newly caged
canary birds—amused, not yet afraid.

A golden anniversary came around
where toasts were made and laughing stories told.
The lovers joined the laugh, although they found
the joke, but not themselves, was growing old.

She started losing and forgetting things.
Where had she left her book, put down her comb?
Her thoughts were like balloons with broken strings.

Daily he visited the nursing home
to make her smile and keep her in their game.
Death came at last. But old age never came.

Lost Daughters

They vanish on their way to school.
A love of reading is their crime.
They're bound to serve a different rule

in marriage long before their time.
(They may be wives, they may be slaves.)
The parents have no strength to climb

from pits that are their daughters' graves.
They keep their younger girls inside.
A girl is safe if she behaves

herself and never seeks a ride
to classes that may fill her head
with words that teach her not to hide

but to respect herself instead.
A daughter mustn't be a fool.
So many lost, so many dead—
they vanish on their way to school.

Passion Spent

My heart, an old and tired cat,
surveying age's box of toys,
will not uncurl itself for that.

Although the mice are slow and fat
and weakened by avoirdupois,
my heart, an old and tired cat,

no longer dreams of mouse or rat,
and if assailed by sudden noise
will not uncurl itself for that.

A hundred arks on Ararat,
the horses of a thousand Troys—
my heart, an old and tired cat

spurns hero's crown and cardinal's hat,
and whether love's for girls or boys
will not uncurl itself for that.

In time the best champagne is flat,
at last the finest banquet cloys.
My heart, an old and tired cat,
will not uncurl itself for that.

Anecdotal Evidence

My aunt who brought her kidney function back
by eating grapefruit seeds for fifty days
makes no impression on our local quack.
It's anecdotal evidence, he says.
There are no reproducible results.
Another person might eat grapefruit seeds
for fifty days and cease to have a pulse.
Cause and effect's the evidence he needs.

The evidence is all in favor of
the proposition that the dead are dead,
despite our bitter hope and wistful love.
Yet when my mother died, my father said
that just before the chill that would not thaw,
her face lit up with joy at what she saw.

Memory Aids

This is the paper that gives the date.
This is the kettle to boil the water.
This is a china breakfast plate.
This is a note to call my daughter.

This is coffee, I drink it black.
This is toast, and I eat it plain.
These are the thoughts I keep on track
to hurry them through my daughter's brain.

These are the things I need to say
to sound as usual on the phone.
The longer I keep my child at bay,
the longer my life is still my own.

How I Spend My Time Since You Died

Mondays, I start a letter. I read through
my notes on everything that happened last week.
I skip the sports news, which didn't interest
you except for Manchester United.

Tuesdays, I brood about
the existence of God and the soul.
If I didn't limit this to one day,
it could take over the entire week.

Wednesdays, I do the week's shopping,
buying foods I couldn't get you to eat.
Afternoons, I watch movies you'd have hated.
Evenings, I work on the letter.

Thursdays, I visualize heaven.
It's partly the gold mosaics of Saint Mark's Cathedral,
combined with an English village
and a dash of Mardi Gras.

Fridays, I deal with my rage.
Saturdays, I go out to dinner,
learning to be unafraid
of a table for one.
I'm not a recluse, after all.

Sundays, I deliver my letter. I place it
among the twisted roots of an oak tree.
An armadillo there, a friend of mine,
will bring it through the roots to you.

Post Diagnosis

So now they know. She, and not he, will say
who gets the cuckoo clock, will give away
the books, the silverware. So much to give
from two shared lives. But only one will live.

His picture of her future (tender, brave,
devoted) always ends beside his grave.
When his life ends, he feels—and she concurs—
nothing will go on happening in hers.

But time will pass and help her to forget,
and while he sees an infinite regret
in that remote expression on her face,
she plans new uses for his closet space.

Life Went on without Her

Just as before, only she wasn't there.
He'd read the news aloud for sixty years
and now he read the headlines to the air,
as though she heard him with angelic ears.

He made the bed, but only used one side.
He never dreamed of her, but every day
she seemed too close to life to be denied.
He set two plates and then took one away.

He learned to cook his meals and sweep the floor,
fold up his socks and organize his ties.
And life went on without her as before,
only she wasn't there to strangers' eyes.

After She Died

Her clothes took on a strange significance
without her standing in the door to choose
among the ranks of dresses, skirts, and pants,
the shelf of hats, the tidy rows of shoes.

Her body wasn't there, although he tried
to see it in the dark. He never found
the hangers parted by her hand, the slide
of some unwanted garment to the ground.

The clothes began to haunt him like a ghost.
They huddled in the closet, gathering
infernal strength, till from the innermost
recess the vampire clothes were whispering
"Her flesh was mortal. We are here to stay."

He couldn't wait to give them all away.

Old Lovers

Old lovers sleep in double beds.
They do not need much space to sleep.
With curve of arms and bend of legs
they shape themselves for dreaming deep.

Old lovers feel each other's breath
as ships in harbor feel the tide,
a subtle current underneath
that pulls them to each other's side.

Old lovers know each other's touch.
Even in sleep the warmth is there,
lifting the mind's unconscious latch,
bridging the intervening air.

Old lovers wake in double beds,
narrow, but still with room for two.
They rise and kiss with graying heads,
ready to see the last years through.

A Visit on All Saints Day

Hello. I've brought your favorite flowers again.
How is it going under there, my dead?
On this side, we're no better off than when
you walked beside us. (Yes, I know I said
the same last year.) The human race is not
improvable. Ask any saint you meet.
We've gone to war again without a thought.
Our leaders shuffle bribes, our heroes cheat.
Your children haven't turned out awfully well,
but who expected it? You're not to blame,
and anyway, I don't believe in hell.
Goodbye for now. I'm always glad I came.
I make no promises about next year,
but one way or another, I'll be here.

Death of My Old Maid Aunt

My great-aunt warned me about men
in theater seats when I was ten
and always in a house or car
to notice where the exits are,
to carry bus fare in my purse
and watch for Peeping Toms or worse.
I laughed a bit, not knowing then
there are worse things to fear than men.
It was my aunt who found instead
a tall dark stranger in her bed.
And now, in all the world of chance,
what heart so dauntless as my aunt's?
She keeps a house where fear is dumb,
and neither thieves nor lovers come.

Diagnosis Day

What happens underneath the skin
has never held my interest long.
The brain I keep my couplets in,
the muscles that set down the song,
were well-oiled parts of my machine.
But now the hand is clumsy thumbs.
To find out what my numbness means,
I lie in state, the scanner hums,
and to its energies I pray
that love prevails, the demon sleeps.
Too soon I hear an intern say
the words my memory overleaps:
a single cell has gone berserk.
And now my death begins its work.

Chemo Day

My doctors are the Borgia popes
whose poison rattles in my veins.
I've laid aside a layman's hopes,
but faith in magic still remains.
If only half my blood is killed
(assuming it's the deadly half),
my inner cup can be refilled
and living gets the final laugh.
But if one vagabond escapes
to multiply his loathly kind,
my death can take a thousand shapes
that leave no exit for my mind.
I run the maze, I scan the map:
my thoughts the prey, my flesh the trap.

Hospice Day

Mouse-like and meek, I've spent my days
in faltering attempts to cope,
awaking from the chemo haze
to find no doorway labeled "Hope."
But I no longer race to win.
A stealthy fog enfolds my brain.
I'm more than fashionably thin,
a pencil sharpened fine by pain.
Here is a door. I knock and ring.
The effort makes me short of breath.
It isn't hope who lets me in.
Beyond this door is only death,
no longer by a thousand cuts,
but guillotine. The future shuts.

An Absence

No one can cry forever, and the world
we live in thinks our grief should be discreet,
not violent like a pitcher's fast ball hurled
into the stands. Our culture favors neat
solutions—counseling, group therapy,
physical workouts, nothing from the gut,
all head-work—lacking the simplicity
of cures for cancer: poison, burn, and cut.

I wouldn't disappoint my friends—who care
what happens next, whose expectations are
that I'll move forward, more or less the same.
I give no trouble, having learned to bear
my loss of you well-covered, like the scar
that was a breast before the surgeons came.

At the Burial of an Abbess

Under the pine trees and the snow,
black on white, and row on row,
we leave our sisters when they go.

We age and die, we fill our space
and no one younger takes our place.
What a mysterious thing is grace

that makes us willing to be gone,
forgotten in our soundless lawn,
even the Order passing on.

Whatever good we might have done
is like the prints where foxes run,
lost when the snow melts in the sun.

But what we've learned above the ground
is to love silence more than sound,
white more than any color found.

The work of all our lifetime lets
us look on death with no regrets:
we vanish as the snow forgets.

measure press . com

formal poetry

on line - Raintown Review)
semi-annual
formal / metrical poetry

Gail White has published three previous books of poetry *(The Price of Everything, Easy Marks* and *The Accidental Cynic)* and several chapbooks, the latest being *Sonnets in a Hostile World.* She has edited three anthologies, including coediting *The Muse Strikes Back.* Gail is widely published and her poetry has appeared in such journals as 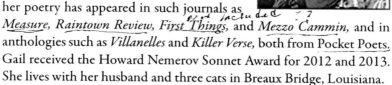 *Measure, Raintown Review, First Things,* and *Mezzo Cammin,* and in anthologies such as *Villanelles* and *Killer Verse,* both from Pocket Poets. Gail received the Howard Nemerov Sonnet Award for 2012 and 2013. She lives with her husband and three cats in Breaux Bridge, Louisiana.

Asperity Steet is a special honoree of the 2014 Able Muse Book Award.

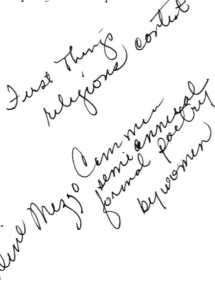

ALSO FROM ABLE MUSE PRESS

William Baer, *Times Square and Other Stories*

Melissa Balmain, *Walking in on People – Poems*

Ben Berman, *Strange Borderlands – Poems*

Michael Cantor, *Life in the Second Circle – Poems*

Catherine Chandler, *Lines of Flight – Poems*

William Conelly, *Uncontested Grounds – Poems*

Maryann Corbett,
    Credo for the Checkout Line in Winter – Poems

John Philip Drury, *Sea Level Rising – Poems*

D.R. Goodman, *Greed: A Confession – Poems*

Margaret Ann Griffiths,
    Grasshopper – The Poetry of M A Griffiths

Jan D. Hodge, *Taking Shape – carmina figurata*

Ellen Kaufman, *House Music – Poems*

Carol Light, *Heaven from Steam – Poems*

April Lindner, *This Bed Our Bodies Shaped – Poems*

Martin McGovern, *Bad Fame – Poems*

Jeredith Merrin, *Cup – Poems*

Richard Newman,
    All the Wasted Beauty of the World – Poems

Frank Osen, *Virtue, Big as Sin – Poems*

Alexander Pepple (Editor), *Able Muse Anthology*

Alexander Pepple (Editor),
    Able Muse – a review of poetry, prose & art
    (semiannual issues, Winter 2010 onward)

James Pollock, *Sailing to Babylon – Poems*

Aaron Poochigian, *The Cosmic Purr – Poems*

John Ridland,
    Sir Gawain and the Green Knight – Translation

Stephen Scaer, *Pumpkin Chucking – Poems*

Hollis Seamon, *Corporeality – Stories*

Carrie Shipers, *Embarking on Catastrophe – Poems*

Matthew Buckley Smith,
    Dirge for an Imaginary World – Poems

Barbara Ellen Sorensen,
    Compositions of the Dead Playing Flutes – Poems

Wendy Videlock, *Slingshots and Love Plums – Poems*

Wendy Videlock, *The Dark Gnu and Other Poems*

Wendy Videlock, *Nevertheless – Poems*

Richard Wakefield, *A Vertical Mile – Poems*

Chelsea Woodard, *Vellum – Poems*

www.ablemusepress.com

CPSIA information can be obtained at www.ICGtesting.com
Printed in the USA
LVOW10s1129200516

489226LV00003B/51/P